Things to Know About Credit Card Chargebacks

First published by Kjøller 2023

Disclaimer:

The information contained in this book is provided for general informational purposes only. While every effort has been made to ensure that the information is accurate and up-to-date, The Author makes no representations or warranties of any kind, express or implied, about the completeness, accuracy, reliability, suitability, or availability with respect to the information, products, services, or related graphics contained in the book for any purpose.

The Author disclaims any liability for any loss or damage, including without limitation, indirect or consequential loss or damage, or any loss or damage whatsoever arising from loss of data or profits arising out of, or in connection with, the use of this book.

Readers are solely responsible for determining the appropriateness of the information contained in this book for their specific purposes and should seek professional advice before acting upon any information contained herein. The Author shall not be liable for any damages of any kind arising from the use of this book or the information contained herein.

Table of Contents

Introduction

As credit card usage continues to rise, so do the frequency of chargebacks. Whether you're a small business owner or a consumer, knowing the ins and outs of chargebacks is crucial. Understanding what chargebacks are, the reasons behind disputes, and the steps to take when one occurs are essential for keeping your finances intact. In "Things to Know about Credit Card Chargebacks," we'll delve into these topics, share expert insights, and provide practical tips to help you navigate the chargeback process with ease. Whether you're a merchant or a buyer, this book is an indispensable resource for protecting your bottom line. So, let's dive in and learn everything there is to know about credit card chargebacks!

Account Updater

A service provided by the major credit card networks that automatically updates the cardholder's account information with merchants, such as new credit card numbers or expiration dates. Account updater services can help reduce the risk of chargebacks resulting from outdated or inaccurate account information.

Accounting Date

The date on which a credit card transaction is settled and funds are transferred from the cardholder's account to the merchant's account. The accounting date may differ from the transaction date, which is the date on which the transaction was initiated.

Acquirer

The financial institution that processes credit card transactions on behalf of the merchant. In a chargeback situation, the acquirer serves as the intermediary between the merchant and card issuer to resolve the dispute.

Acquirer Fee

A fee charged by the acquirer for processing credit card transactions on behalf of the merchant. Acquirer fees may be a flat fee per transaction or a percentage of the transaction amount.

Acquiring Bank

The bank or financial institution that receives the credit card transaction from the merchant's bank or payment processor. The acquiring bank processes the transaction and deposits the funds into the merchant's account.

Address Verification System (AVS)

A fraud prevention tool that compares the billing address provided by the cardholder with the address on file at the card issuer. Merchants can use AVS to reduce the risk of chargebacks resulting from fraudulent transactions.

Affiliate

 A company or individual that promotes another company's products or services in exchange for a commission on sales. In the context of chargebacks, affiliates may be held liable for chargebacks related to sales they referred to the merchant.

Affiliate Network

A group of affiliates that work together to promote a particular product or service. Merchants often use affiliate networks to expand their reach and increase sales. However, affiliate networks can also increase the risk of chargebacks if the affiliates engage in fraudulent or deceptive practices.

Anti-Fraud Tools

Tools and technologies employed by merchants and payment processors to reduce the risk of fraudulent transactions and chargebacks. Anti-fraud tools may include fraud detection algorithms, address verification systems, and 3D Secure authentication.

Arbitration

A process in which a chargeback dispute is resolved by a neutral third party. Both the merchant and card issuer submit evidence to an arbitration panel, which makes a final decision on the dispute.

Association

The credit card networks, such as Visa and Mastercard, that set the rules and policies governing credit card transactions. Merchants must abide by the association's guidelines to accept credit card payments.

Association Chargeback

A chargeback initiated by a credit card association, such as Visa or Mastercard, rather than by the cardholder or the merchant. Association chargebacks are typically the result of a violation of the association's rules and regulations.

Authentication

The process of verifying the identity of the cardholder during a credit card transaction. Authentication may involve requiring the cardholder to enter a PIN or provide additional identifying information.

Authorization

The process of obtaining approval from the card issuer to process a transaction. If a transaction is not authorized, it will be declined and not processed.

Authorization Code

A unique code generated by the card issuer when a credit card transaction is approved. The authorization code confirms that the cardholder has sufficient credit available to complete the transaction and that the transaction is not fraudulent.

Authorization hold

A temporary hold placed on a cardholder's account to ensure that funds are available to cover a transaction. An authorization hold is typically released when the transaction is completed or cancelled.

Automated Clearing House (ACH)

A network used for electronic fund transfers between banks in the United States. ACH transactions are often used for direct deposit of payroll, government benefits, and tax refunds.

AVS (Address Verification Service)

A fraud prevention tool that verifies the cardholder's billing address by comparing it to the address on file with the card issuer. AVS can be used to reduce the risk of fraud and chargebacks.

Card Issuing Bank

The Card Issuing Bank is the organization that issues a credit card. This bank is responsible for authorizing transactions and is the first point of contact when a chargeback is initiated.

Card Not Present (CNP) fraud

Card Not Present (CNP) fraud is a type of fraud where a credit card is used to make purchases online or over the phone without the physical presence of the cardholder. This type of fraud makes chargebacks more prevalent, as the cardholder may not have authorized the transaction.

Cardholder

The individual or entity that owns and uses the credit card. In a chargeback situation, the cardholder initiates the dispute with the issuer.

Cardholder Information Security

Cardholder Information Security is the implementation of security measures to protect payment card information from unauthorized access, theft, and fraudulent activities. Compliance with data security standards can help merchants provide a more secure online experience and avoid chargebacks.

Chargeback

A transaction dispute initiated by the cardholder with their card issuer. Chargebacks can occur for a variety of reasons, such as fraud, goods not received, or a product or service not as described. The merchant typically has a limited time to respond to the chargeback and provide evidence to dispute it.

Chargeback Dispute

A Chargeback Dispute is a process where a merchant seeks to dispute a chargeback initiated by a cardholder. Merchants who win the dispute retain the payment and avoid the chargeback.

Chargeback Ratio

Chargeback Ratio is the ratio between the total number of chargebacks and the total number of processed transactions. A high chargeback ratio can result in the loss of the merchant account and increase negative impact on reputation.

Chargeback Reason Codes

Chargeback Reason Codes are unique codes used by banks or credit card issuers to indicate the specific reason for a chargeback. Reason codes can include fraud, billing errors, or disputes over the quality of goods or services received, and the code chosen determines which party is responsible for the chargeback.

Chargeback Representment

Chargeback Representment is the process of a merchant providing evidence to dispute a chargeback. This evidence can include receipts, tracking information, and correspondence with the cardholder, and helps merchants reclaim funds that were taken due to a chargeback.

Collaboration

Collaboration between merchants and payment processors is essential in ensuring effective chargeback management. Payment processors can provide data analytics to help merchants reduce chargebacks, and merchants can provide feedback to payment processors to help improve fraud detection tools.

Compliance

Compliance with credit card regulations, such as the Payment Card Industry Data Security Standards (PCI DSS), is crucial in reducing the risk of chargebacks. Non-compliance can result in fines, liability for stolen card data, and loss of customers' trust.

Contract

A Contract is an agreement between a merchant and a cardholder for the delivery of goods or services. Contracts that are not fulfilled can lead to chargebacks.

Conviction

Conviction refers to a merchant's obligation to validate the quality of goods or services that they provide to the cardholder. Merchants who don't deliver what was promised can face convictions, which lead to chargebacks and negative impact on their reputation.

Credit

Credit refers to the reversal of a transaction,where funds are returned to the cardholder's account. Credit is usually issued when goods or services were not delivered, or the cardholder was billed incorrectly.

Customer Dispute

Customer Dispute is a chargeback initiated by a cardholder who disputes a transaction made on their credit card. Customer Disputes can result from issues such as product quality, shipping delays, and incorrect charges.

Customer Service

The quality of customer service provided by merchants plays a crucial role in reducing chargebacks. Proper communication, dispute resolution, and refunds can help merchants to retain customers and avoid chargebacks.

E-commerce fraud

E-commerce fraud is any type of fraud that takes place during an online transaction. It usually involves a stolen credit card being used to make a purchase, followed by a chargeback request by the cardholder. This can be difficult to prevent, so online merchants should consider using fraud prevention tools to help reduce their risk.

EMV

EMV refers to the chip technology used in credit cards. It stands for Europay, Mastercard, and Visa, which are the companies that developed the standard. EMV cards are more secure than traditional magnetic stripe cards because they generate unique codes for each transaction, making it much harder for fraudsters to steal card information.

Financial Institution

A bank or any other entity that provides financial services, such as issuing credit cards, processing payments, settling disputes, or underwriting loans.

Fine Print

The terms and conditions of a contract that are not clearly visible or easy to understand. In the context of credit card chargebacks, fine print can refer to the terms of service or user agreement that governs the relationship between the merchant, the processor, and the card issuer.

FITD Rule

The "FedEx In Time Delivery" rule is a guideline that merchants use to protect themselves from chargebacks due to late deliveries. It implies that if a merchant can prove that the item was shipped and delivered on time, they can dispute any chargebacks related to delays or non-delivery.

Floor Limit

The maximum dollar amount that a merchant is allowed to authorize for a credit card transaction without obtaining prior approval from the card issuer. This limit varies by transaction type, merchant category, card type, and other factors.

Forced Refund

A type of chargeback where the card issuer forces the merchant to refund a disputed transaction, even if the merchant believes it was legitimate. This can happen due to regulatory requirements, internal policies, or disputes between the card issuer and the merchant.

Fraud Detection

The process of identifying and preventing fraudulent activities by using various software tools, algorithms, or manual reviews. This can include monitoring for suspicious patterns, unusual behaviors, or risky transactions.

Fraudulent Chargeback

A type of chargeback where the cardholder disputes a legitimate transaction, claiming not to have authorized it. This can happen due to unauthorized access to the card account, repeated use of a card by someone else, or false claims of lost/stolen cards.

Fraudulent Merchant

A merchant who engages in fraudulent activities, such as selling counterfeit goods, charging unauthorized fees, or misrepresenting the quality or features of their products/ services. Fraudulent merchants can cause chargebacks, legal disputes, and reputational damage to themselves and their partners.

Friendly Fraud

A type of chargeback where the cardholder disputes a legitimate transaction, but it is not caused by any criminal activity. This can happen due to lack of communication, misunderstandings, forgetfulness, or deliberate deception.

Fulfillment

The process of delivering goods or services to customers in accordance with their orders. This includes packaging, shipping, tracking, and delivering the products/ services.

Glossary of terms

A list of all the technical terms related to credit card chargebacks that are frequently used in articles or in discussions about the topic.

Hierarchy of Representments

This describes the flow of chargeback disputes between cardholders, merchants, and banks. A chargeback first goes from a cardholder to their bank, who sends it to the merchant's bank. The merchant's bank may then return the dispute to the merchant to gather evidence to fight the chargeback, before finally responding to the cardholder's bank with either an acceptance or dispute of the chargeback.

High Risk Merchant

This is a merchant whose business is deemed to pose a higher risk of chargebacks and fraud, such as those dealing in adult content or gambling. These merchants may have stricter guidelines for processing payments, such as higher fees or reserves, to mitigate risk to the banks.

Holdback Reserve

A holdback reserve is a portion of a merchant's sales that a bank withholds in case of future chargebacks or losses. This reserve can be used to cover fees or costs associated with chargebacks, and is typically returned to the merchant after a certain period or with no chargeback activity.

Honeypot Account

A honeypot account is a fake account set up by a merchant to "catch" fraudsters attempting to make fraudulent purchases. Any suspicious transactions on the honeypot allow the merchant to gather evidence and prevent future chargebacks or losses.

Issuer

The financial institution that issues the credit card to the cardholder. In a chargeback situation, the issuer represents the cardholder and is responsible for initiating the chargeback.

JCB

JCB is a credit card company based in Japan, and it is one of the four largest credit card companies globally. In the U.S., JCB credit cards are infrequently used, but merchants should still take the time to understand the chargeback rules related to JCB card usage.

Keyed Transactions

This describes the process of manually entering a customer's credit card information, rather than swiping or dipping the card. Keyed transactions are typically used when a physical card is unavailable, such as with online shopping or over the phone purchases. They can also be initiated when the magnetic stripe on a card is damaged or unreadable.

Keyed-in Card

This refers to a credit or debit card number that is manually typed in, rather than swiped or dipped. Keyed-in cards are most commonly used in situations where the physical card is not available, such as for online transactions or phone orders.

Kiosk Fraud

This type of fraud is when a hacker installs a device or software in an automated kiosk machine to capture credit card information from customers who use the machine. The hacker can then use the stolen credit card details to make unauthorized purchases or withdraw funds from the customer's account without their knowledge or consent. Kiosk fraud can occur at any type of automated machine, including ATMs, self-checkout lanes in supermarkets, and gas pumps.

Kiting

This is a type of fraud that involves moving funds between two or more bank accounts in order to artificially inflate the balances of those accounts. Kiting is typically used to create the illusion of high account balances, which can then be used to obtain loans and credit that the fraudster would not otherwise qualify for.

Know Your Customer (KYC)

This refers to the process of verifying the identity of a customer and their financial history. KYC is a critical component of anti-money laundering (AML) regulations and is mandatory for banks and financial institutions. It involves collecting and analyzing personal information, such as the customer's name, address, and social security number, to determine the potential risk of doing business with them. The KYC process helps prevent financial crimes, such as fraud and money laundering.

Knowledge of Cardholder

This is a term used when a merchant has received a chargeback, and the issuing bank wants to know if the person who used the card was authorized to do so. The merchant is required to provide evidence that they obtained the card from the legitimate cardholder and that the transaction was authorized.

Knowledge-Based Authentication

This is a method of verifying a customer's identity by asking them a series of questions that only they should know the answer to, such as their mother's maiden name or the make and model of their first car. Knowledge-based authentication is often used to add an extra layer of security to high-risk transactions, such as transferring large sums of money or opening a new credit card account.

Knowledge-Based Authentication (KBA)

This is a security technique used to verify the identity of an individual or entity by requiring them to answer a series of questions based on personal information only they should know. KBA is frequently used in financial transactions to prevent fraud and protect the security of sensitive information.

Knowledge-Driven Authentication

This is a method of verifying a customer's identity that uses biometric or behavioral data, such as a fingerprint or voice pattern, to confirm that the person is who they claim to be. Knowledge-driven authentication is a more secure alternative to traditional password-based authentication, which can be easily hacked and is vulnerable to phishing scams. It is commonly used in industries that require a high level of security, such as financial services and healthcare.

Late Delivery Chargeback

A dispute initiated by a cardholder regarding a purchase that was not delivered on time, as promised by the merchant. This type of chargeback can be avoided by clearly communicating delivery expectations to customers.

Late Presentment

This occurs when a merchant waits too long to present a charge to the issuer. In such cases, the issuer may not honor the charge, leading to a potential chargeback.

Late Submission

A late submission is a chargeback response that is sent after the deadline for submissions. It can result in an automatic loss of the chargeback dispute.

Legitimate Charge

A term used to describe a charge that is valid and authorized. Cardholders will not dispute a legitimate charge.

Legitimate Chargeback

A chargeback that is initiated by a legitimate cardholder, typically due to a billing error or a product/service that was not as described.

Letter of Authorization

A written document that gives permission to someone for a specific action. It is commonly used in the authorization process for a chargeback. A letter of authorization should include details such as the cardholder's name, the transaction amount, and the reason for requesting the chargeback.

Letter of Retrieval (LOR)

A letter of retrieval is a request from the issuing bank to the acquiring bank or merchant for additional information regarding a transaction. It's usually the first step in the chargeback process.

Letter of Review

A process by which a merchant can challenge a chargeback by providing additional information or evidence to the issuer. This can be a critical step for merchants to recover lost revenue.

Liability Limits

Specific limits imposed on merchants by credit card companies for chargebacks. If a merchant goes above their liability limit, they may be suspended from accepting credit card payments altogether.

Liability Shift

The term refers to the transfer of financial responsibility from the merchant to the card issuer in a chargeback dispute. After the liability shift, the card issuer bears the financial loss incurred due to the chargeback. This shift usually happens when a merchant fails to comply with the card issuer's rules and regulations.

Liability Waiver

A contractual agreement in which one party agrees to assume responsibility for certain events or situations. In the context of chargebacks, it may be used to shift responsibility to the cardholder for unauthorized transactions.

Lien

A legal claim placed on a merchant's funds or property. A lien can be placed on a merchant's account in the case of a chargeback dispute.

Limited Chargeback

A chargeback with a predetermined time limit for disputes to be filed. After the limit has passed, the disputed charge is deemed valid.

Limited Chargeback Rights

This term refers to the limited options that merchants have in responding to chargeback disputes. Merchants are often at a disadvantage as card issuers tend to favor their cardholders in chargeback disputes.

Limited Liability

Limited liability refers to the merchant's liability in a chargeback dispute. Merchants are not usually held responsible if they provide valid proof that the transaction was authorized.

Limited Reason Code

A reason code used by card issuers to categorize a chargeback. It helps the merchant understand the reason for the dispute and respond accordingly.

Limited Recourse

A specific type of chargeback that applies to cardholders who have been scammed or defrauded by merchants. It limits the cardholder's recourse to the amount initially charged.

Login Credentials

The combination of a username and password used for authentication when accessing a website or other online service. It is crucial for merchants to keep login credentials secure to avoid potential chargebacks from fraudulent activity.

Long Story Short

An informal expression used to quickly summarize a situation. However, in the context of chargebacks, it can be important for merchants to provide detailed explanations of transactions to avoid potential chargebacks.

Long-Tail Liability

Refers to the length of time a merchant can potentially be held responsible for a chargeback. The length depends on the card issuer's policies and regulations.

Loss Ratio

A metric used by credit card issuers to evaluate the risk of chargebacks. It is calculated by dividing the number of chargebacks by the total value of transactions made.

Loss Recovery

This term refers to the process by which a merchant recovers the loss incurred in a chargeback dispute. Merchants typically file a dispute with the issuing bank to reclaim the lost funds. If the chargeback is successful, the loss recovery process may involve a chargeback reversal, debt collection or insurance claims.

Lost Refund Override

A feature offered by some merchant account providers that allows merchants to override and re-process a refund for a transaction that was previously charged back. This can be useful for merchants who wish to fight an illegitimate chargeback.

Lost/Stolen Chargeback

A chargeback initiated by a cardholder for a transaction they claim was made without their authorization due to a lost or stolen card.

Magnetic Stripe

The black strip on the back of a credit card that contains the cardholder's information. Magnetic stripes are used to process credit card payments when the card is swiped through a card reader.

Mandatory arbitration

Mandatory arbitration refers to a contractual agreement between a merchant and a payment processor that requires disputes to be resolved through arbitration rather than through the court system.

Manual credit card imprint

A manual credit card imprint refers to the process of manually imprinting credit card information onto paper using a credit card imprinter. This method is typically used when a merchant is unable to process the transaction through an electronic terminal.

Mastercard

A global payment network that allows consumers and businesses to securely make credit card transactions.

Mastercard SecureCode

A security feature used by Mastercard to protect cardholders from fraudulent transactions. Mastercard SecureCode requires the cardholder to verify their identity by entering a unique code, in addition to their credit card number, when making purchases online.

Match

Stands for "Member Alert to Control High-risk" and refers to a program designed to prevent fraudulent activity by monitoring potential high-risk merchants. If a merchant is identified as high-risk, their payment processor may require them to adhere to additional security protocols or may limit their access to certain payment methods.

Merchandise return

Merchandise return occurs when a customer returns a product to the merchant. Merchants must have a clear return policy in place, including procedures for issuing refunds, restocking fees, and timelines.

Merchant

A business or individual that accepts credit card payments as a form of payment for goods or services. Merchants are responsible for ensuring that their customers' payment information is kept safe and secure.

Merchant Account

A type of bank account that allows businesses to accept credit card payments. Merchant accounts are established through an agreement between the merchant, the acquiring bank, and the payment processor.

Merchant acquirer

A merchant acquirer is a financial institution that provides merchant accounts to businesses. Acquirers are responsible for processing credit card transactions and facilitating the transfer of funds between the merchant and the issuing bank.

Merchant Category Code

A four-digit code assigned to merchants by credit card companies that identifies the type of goods or services they offer.

Micro-charges

Micro-charges refer to small transactions that are made on a credit card, typically less than $1. These charges are often used to verify the cardholder's identity and are sometimes used fraudulently.

Microtransaction

A small payment or financial transaction, usually valued at less than $1. Microtransactions are often used to purchase digital goods or services, such as apps or music downloads, and are becoming increasingly popular in the mobile payments industry.

Mid-Qualification

A term used to describe credit card processing rates that fall between qualified and non-qualified rates. Mid-qualification rates apply to transactions that meet some, but not all, of the criteria for the qualified rate. These transactions typically involve rewards cards or transactions that are manually keyed in by the merchant.

Mid-Qualified Transaction

A mid-qualified transaction refers to a credit card transaction that does not qualify for the lowest processing rates. This may occur if the transaction is made with a higher-risk credit card or if the transaction is not processed correctly by the merchant.

Minimum Chargeback Rate

The percentage of transactions that result in a chargeback within a specific time period. Merchants are typically required to maintain a minimum chargeback rate to avoid fines or penalties.

Minimum transaction fee

A minimum transaction fee is a fee charged by the payment processor for processing transactions below a certain amount. This fee is applied to each transaction that falls below the specified minimum amount.

Misrepresentation

Misrepresentation occurs when a merchant provides false information about a product or service or misrepresents the terms of a transaction. Misrepresentation can lead to chargebacks and other legal issues.

Mitigation

Mitigation refers to the process of reducing or lessening the impact of a chargeback on a merchant's business. This involves providing compelling evidence to the issuing bank to prove the validity of the transaction.

Monthly statement

A monthly statement details all credit card transactions processed during the statement period. Merchants should review their monthly statements for accuracy and ensure that all disputes are resolved in a timely manner.

Offender

A term used to describe a customer who files chargebacks in bad faith, in an attempt to commit fraud or abuse the chargeback system. Merchants can use chargeback representment to hold these offenders accountable for their actions.

Ombudsman

A third-party intermediary who helps resolve disputes between cardholders and merchants during the chargeback process. The ombudsman will investigate the issue and provide a resolution that is acceptable to both parties.

Online Dispute Resolution (ODR)

A platform used to resolve disputes between merchants and customers online. ODR systems can save time and resources by allowing parties to negotiate a resolution without the need for a formal legal process.

Operating Fee

A fee charged by the credit card network for processing credit card transactions. The fee is based on a percentage of the transaction amount and is used to cover the network's operating costs. Merchants can factor operating fees into their pricing strategy to ensure profitability.

Operating Regulations

A set of rules that govern the processes and procedures used by credit card networks. Merchants and banks must comply with these regulations when processing credit card transactions to avoid penalties or fines.

Order Confirmation

A document, such as an email or receipt, confirming that the customer placed an order with the merchant. It includes the date, amount, and the products or services purchased.

Order Fulfillment

The process by which a merchant completes an order and delivers the product or service to the customer. Proper order fulfillment can reduce the likelihood of chargebacks due to product delivery issues.

Ordinary Course of Business

A term used to describe a transaction that is consistent with the merchant's regular course of business. Chargebacks filed for transactions that fall within the ordinary course of business are less likely to be successful.

Out-of-Policy Chargeback

A chargeback that is filed outside the timeframe or reason codes allowed by the credit card network's policies. Merchants can dispute these chargebacks if they are not legitimate or outside the policy.

Overreliance

A situation where a merchant relies too much on friendly fraud detection and prevention tools and fails to address genuine chargeback issues. Overreliance can lead to a higher chargeback rate and financial losses for the merchant.

Partial Chargeback

A disputed transaction that is only partially refunded to the customer.

Payment Gateway

A payment gateway is a software application that facilitates online credit and debit card transactions. It encrypts sensitive information and securely sends it to the payment processor for authorization and settlement. Payment gateways are often used in e-commerce businesses and can be integrated into shopping carts, mobile applications, and virtual terminals.

Payment Processor

A payment processor is a third-party entity that handles transactions between a merchant and a customer's bank for credit or debit card transactions. The payment processor ensures that funds are transferred securely and in a timely manner. They also verify transactions for fraud and process chargebacks if necessary. In the event of a chargeback, the payment processor will communicate with the issuing bank to retrieve evidence and process the dispute.

Penalty Fees

Fees assessed by the processor or issuing bank for merchant's causing excessive chargebacks or fraud.

Permanent Account Number (PAN)

A permanent account number (PAN) is a unique identifier assigned to a credit or debit card. It consists of 16 digits and is used to identify the issuing bank, account holder, and account type. The PAN is also used to authorize transactions and process payments. Merchants are required to store the PAN securely and follow strict security protocols to protect customer data.

Point of Interaction (POI)

The place where a customer initiates or authorizes an electronic payment transaction.

Point of Sale (POS)

The location or device where the customer swipes, inserts, or taps their card to make a payment.

POS Terminal

A point-of-sale (POS) terminal is a device used to process credit and debit card transactions at a physical location, like a store or restaurant. It interacts with the payment processor to authorize the transaction, capture funds, and transmit instructions to the merchant bank. A POS terminal can come in many forms, including a stand-alone device, a tablet or mobile device, or an integrated system that also manages inventory and customer data.

Pre-Arbitration

Pre-arbitration is a process used in the chargeback process if the initial dispute resolution is unsuccessful. The transaction is escalated to pre-arbitration, and the issuing bank and acquiring bank attempt to resolve the dispute through arbitration. Pre-arbitration is a more formal process that involves legal representation and can be costly for merchants if they are found liable for the dispute.

Presentment

Presentment is the process of supplying evidence and documentation to support the merchant's case in a chargeback dispute. The merchant is required to provide compelling evidence that the transaction was valid and authorized by the customer. Presentment can be done through the payment processor's dispute resolution system, and the outcome is decided by the issuing bank. Failure to provide sufficient evidence can result in a loss for the merchant.

Preventative Action Plan

A plan established by the merchant to prevent future disputes and chargebacks, including improving customer service or updating accounting systems.

Preventative Measures

Steps taken by the business to reduce the likelihood of disputes, such as improving communication and delivering accurate products or services.

Proactive Monitoring

The system in place by the merchant to monitor the customer's account for any suspicious activity that can lead to a chargeback.

Processing Fees

Fees charged by the processing bank or payment gateway for each transaction processed.

Processor

A third-party vendor that handles the electronic exchange of transaction information, such as authorization and settlement, between the merchant and issuing bank.

Processor Chargeback Fee

A processor chargeback fee is a fee charged to merchants when a customer disputes a transaction and initiates a chargeback. This fee is typically passed on from the payment processor to the merchant for handling the dispute. The fee varies depending on the processor, but it can range from $15 to $100 per chargeback. Merchants may also incur additional fees if they exceed a certain number of chargebacks, which can have a negative impact on their ability to process payments or maintain a merchant account.

Processor Compliance Fee

A processor compliance fee is a fee charged to merchants for ensuring compliance with industry regulations and security standards. This fee is meant to cover the cost of maintaining compliance and mitigating risk for the payment processor. Merchants may be charged annually or quarterly for this fee and are required to take certain steps to maintain compliance, such as regular security audits and training.

Proof of Delivery

A document or receipt that proves a product was physically delivered to the customer.

Proof of Delivery (POD)

Proof of delivery (POD) is a document that shows that a product or service was delivered to the customer. This can include a signature from the customer, a delivery confirmation from a carrier, or a timestamped photo of the delivery location. Merchants are required to keep detailed records of POD to defend against chargebacks that claim the product or service was not delivered.

Proof of Refund

Evidence that the merchant refunded the customer's account, such as a credit to their card or a receipt showing the refund.

Provisional Credit

Provisional credit is a temporary credit issued to a merchant during the chargeback process. The issuing bank provides this credit to the merchant while the investigation is underway. This allows the merchant to maintain adequate cash flow while awaiting the final outcome of the chargeback. The provisional credit may be revoked if the investigation determines that the chargeback is valid.

Purchase Verified

A program that verifies a customer's purchase with the issuing bank to mitigate the risk of chargebacks.

Quality Dispute

A quality dispute is a claim made by a customer that the product or service received was not as described, or the quality was below expectations. Chargebacks can occur due to quality disputes when a merchant fails to resolve the issue to the customer's satisfaction. Customers can initiate a chargeback, which is essentially a refund requested from their card issuer.

Query Response Time

Query response time is the maximum amount of time that a merchant or card issuer takes to respond to a dispute query. The query response time for chargebacks is 45 days for issuers, and merchants have 20 days to respond to a chargeback inquiry.

Reason Code

Reason Code refers to a specific code used by credit card networks such as Visa, Mastercard and more that explains the reason for the chargeback. It can range from fraud, non-receipt of goods, services not rendered, or incorrect billing.

Reasonable Basis

Reasonable Basis is the concept that merchants must have legal and factual evidence supporting their business transactions. This evidence is useful when fighting disputes, where it carries a lot of weight in proving the transaction is legitimate.

Rebuttal

Rebuttal is the process where the merchant can submit evidence to refute the chargeback claim. It is a chance for the merchant to dispute the chargeback and present counter-evidence to win the case.

Recovery

Recovery happens when a merchant is able to recover lost revenue due to chargebacks they previously suffered from. This can be done either by disputing the chargeback via representment or by using a chargeback protection service.

Representment

Representment is a process in which a merchant disputes a chargeback by submitting evidence that justifies the transaction to their acquiring bank. The merchant can also prove that the goods were delivered or the services were rendered, therefore earning back the sale.

Responder

A Respondent refers to the party responsible for responding to a chargeback dispute. This can either be the merchant or the acquiring bank who is responsible for submitting all the evidence supporting the transaction.

Retrieval Fee

A Retrieval fee is charged by the acquirer to the merchant to retrieve copies of transaction documents to help mitigate the risk of a disputed transaction leading to a chargeback at a later date.

Retrieval Period

The Retrieval period is the time available for the acquirer or the merchant to respond to a retrieval request. This can vary between networks but it's generally between 10 and 45 days.

Retrieval Request

A Retrieval Request is sent by the issuing bank to the acquiring bank to ask for the original transaction receipt or documentation pertaining to the transaction in question. It is the first step that initiates the chargeback process.

Return Policy

The Return policy is a merchant's policy that outlines the terms and conditions for returning goods and receiving refunds. Having a clear return policy in place can help merchants reduce the risk of chargebacks.

Technical chargeback

A chargeback that is initiated due to technical errors or glitches during the payment process. These types of chargebacks can often be avoided through proper payment processing procedures.

Termination

The process of terminating a merchant account due to excessive chargebacks or fraudulent activity. Termination can have negative consequences for the merchant's business.

Termination reserve

A specific amount of money that is held in reserve by the acquiring bank to cover any future chargebacks that may occur when a merchant's account is terminated.

Third Party Processor

A third-party processor refers to a company or service that processes transactions on behalf of a merchant. Merchants often use third-party processors to handle the technical and financial aspects of a transaction, including fraud and chargeback management.

Third-party processors

Payment processors that provide services to merchants on behalf of an acquiring bank. These processors can help merchants identify and prevent chargebacks, but they may also charge additional fees.

Threshold

The level of chargebacks that a merchant can receive before their account is at risk of termination. A high chargeback threshold is desirable for merchants.

Time Limits

Time limits refer to the period within which a cardholder must dispute a transaction. Chargebacks can only be initiated within specific time frames, which can vary based on the type of transaction, the issuer or the card network.

Timeframe

The period of time within which a chargeback can be filed. The timeframe varies depending on the credit card issuer and the reason for the chargeback.

Track data

Payment information that is stored and transmitted during a credit card transaction. Track data is used to determine whether a chargeback is valid or fraudulent.

Transaction

The act of making a purchase with a credit card or other payment method. Chargebacks occur when there is a dispute related to a past transaction.

Transaction Amount

Transaction amount refers to the amount charged to the card for a transaction, including taxes, fees and shipping charges. This amount may be the subject of a chargeback if the transaction was unauthorized or improperly processed.

Transaction Authorization

Transaction authorization refers to the process of obtaining approval for a transaction from the issuing bank. Authorization is necessary to ensure that the card has sufficient funds or credit to complete the transaction.

Transaction Code

A transaction code is a unique code that identifies a transaction based on various factors, such as the type of transaction, merchant category code, and the amount of the transaction. This code may be used to identify a transaction during the dispute process.

Transaction Currency

Transaction currency refers to the type of currency used to complete a transaction. A dispute may arise if the transaction was conducted in a different currency than what was advertised or if the exchange rate was not properly disclosed.

Transaction Decline

A transaction decline occurs when a card issuer does not authorize a transaction due to various reasons, such as insufficient funds, credit limit exceeded, or fraud. A transaction decline may be the subject of a chargeback if the cardholder disputes the decision.

Transaction Dispute

A transaction dispute is a request made by a cardholder to their issuing bank to reverse a card transaction. When a transaction dispute is initiated, the bank will investigate the transaction to determine whether it was authorized, completed correctly, and meets the provisions of card network regulations.

Transaction Dispute Reason Code

A transaction dispute reason code is a code used to identify the reason for a transaction dispute. The reason code is used by the card issuer to determine the validity of the dispute and whether a chargeback is warranted.

Transaction Dispute Response

A transaction dispute response is a merchant's response to a transaction dispute initiated by a cardholder. The response will typically include supporting documentation and evidence to support the merchant's position.

Transaction Dispute Rights

Transaction dispute rights refer to the cardholders' rights to dispute a transaction under certain circumstances, such as unauthorized transactions or transactions in which goods or services were not received.

Transaction Processing Error

A transaction processing error refers to any error that occurred during the processing of a transaction that may have resulted in an incorrect or unauthorized charge.

Transaction Protection

Transaction protection refers to measures taken by card issuers, card networks and merchants to protect against fraud and unauthorized transactions.

Transaction Receipt

A transaction receipt is evidence of a card transaction, typically provided as a paper or digital copy by the merchant to the cardholder. Often the receipt will contain details such as date, time, merchant name, location, and the amount of the transaction.

Transaction Risk Assessment

Transaction risk assessment refers to the process of evaluating the level of risk associated with a specific transaction based on various factors such as the transaction amount, merchant category, and the likelihood of fraud. Higher-risk transactions may be subject to additional scrutiny and potentially result in more chargebacks.

Travel services chargebacks

A type of chargeback that is common in the travel industry, typically related to cancelled trips or disputed fees. Proper documentation and communication can help prevent these chargebacks.

True fraud

A type of chargeback that occurs when a credit card is stolen or used without the owner's permission. Merchants may be held liable for true fraud chargebacks if they do not take proper security measures.

Unauthorized Transaction

A transaction made without the account holder's permission is considered an Unauthorized Transaction. If an account holder receives a statement that includes fraudulent transactions, they should immediately report the unauthorized transaction to their card issuer. The issuer will investigate, and if found to have occurred without the account holder's permission, the issuer will issue a chargeback.

Unclear Descriptor

An Unclear Descriptor is a term used to describe a transaction that is unclear or ambiguous. This can occur when a merchant uses a descriptor that is not immediately recognizable to the cardholder, such as using an abbreviated name or code for their business. Where it is unclear or ambiguous, a cardholder may initiate a Chargeback.

Underwriting

Underwriting is a process undertaken by the credit card issuer to determine if an applicant is eligible for a credit card. The process involves assessing the applicant's credit history and income statements, among other considerations. The decision to approve or decline the credit card application is based on the results of the Underwriting process.

Unique Identifier

A Unique Identifier is a code issued by the credit card issuer that is used to identify the credit cardholder. This code is unique to the cardholder and helps to ensure that the cardholder's identity is protected. Unique Identifiers are only used by authorized personnel for the purposes of verification and validation.

Universal Billing Error

Universal Billing Error occurs when an error occurs due to the billing entity. This error sees the customer getting billed an incorrect amount for a product. Once discovered, the customer can pursue a Chargeback.

Unposted Transaction

Unposted Transaction means a transaction that has not yet been completed by the issuer. Typically, this occurs when the payment clearance process takes longer than expected. An example would be a payment made on a weekend or holiday. The payment might not be posted onto the account until the next business day, leading to confusion regarding the transaction.

Unrecoverable Funds

Unrecoverable Funds is a term used when a cardholder has no funds to cover a charge and has no intent to pay the debt. When this happens, the underlying debt is considered Unrecoverable, and the card issuer may initiate a Chargeback to protect themselves.

Upcoding

Upcoding refers to a situation where a merchant falsely marks the price of a product higher than its actual price. This practice is considered fraudulent and may prompt the issuance of a Chargeback upon discovery.

User Error

User Error is when a customer makes an error while making a payment using their credit card, leading to a chargeback being issued. Common mistakes include the wrong card detail, incorrect amount entered, or a duplicate transaction. Thus, customers need to check their transactions carefully to avoid such issues leading to a chargeback.

Utility Chargeback

Utility Chargeback is a term used in the utility sector, where a customer initiates a chargeback for a service fee, such as gas or electricity. Utility companies typically have a set of rules for Chargeback protocols, and the customer needs to follow these to pursue their claim.

Valid Evidence

In a credit card chargeback, valid evidence is any document provided by the merchant to disprove the disputed transaction. This may include receipts, invoices, shipping and delivery documents, or any other evidence that proves the transaction's legitimacy.

Valid Reason Code

A Reason Code is a three-digit number used to identify the type of dispute in a credit card chargeback. The reason code indicates the reason for the dispute's initiation and can be used by the merchant and the cardholder to resolve the issue. A Valid Reason Code is one that meets the specific requirements set by the card network for disputing a transaction.

Vendor

A vendor is a company or individual that sells goods or services to others. In the context of credit card chargebacks, vendors are often the subject of disputes raised by dissatisfied customers.

Vendor Dispute

It is a dispute that arises between a merchant and supplier when the products or services provided do not meet the required specification or quality. Vendor Disputes can lead to chargebacks initiated by the merchant on the supplier's charge account. Merchants may initiate disputes if they receive faulty goods or if the supplier has not fulfilled their part of the agreement in the given time frame.

Venmo

Venmo is a mobile payment service that allows users to pay and receive money from other users. It also offers a chargeback feature that enables users to dispute unauthorized transactions.

Verbal Authorization

It is when a merchant receives authorization to process a transaction verbally instead of through the usual electronic means. A verbal authorization may be necessary when a merchant's device malfunctions or when the card is not present during the transaction. The merchant must be able to provide proof of verbal authorization in case of a dispute.

Verification Code

A Verification Code is a security code provided by credit card companies to help prevent fraud. It is usually a three or four-digit code printed on the back of credit cards.

Verified by Visa

It is a credit card security program offered by Visa to protect cardholders from fraudulent transactions. Verified by Visa adds an additional layer of authentication by requiring the cardholder to enter a password to complete the purchase process. This helps prevent unauthorized access to the cardholder's account.

Vindicated Chargeback

It is a chargeback that has been won by the merchant. If the merchant provides evidence to the bank supporting that the transaction was legitimate or the cardholder withdrew their dispute, the bank will reverse the chargeback, and the funds will be returned to the merchant.

Vindictive Chargeback

This is a fraudulent chargeback initiated by a malicious customer to exact revenge on a merchant. Such chargebacks are usually unfounded and have no merit.

Virtual Terminal

It is a software application enabling merchants to process credit and debit card transactions manually through a website. Virtual terminals require an internet connection to process transactions and usually come with fraud prevention features such as Address Verification System (AVS) and Card Verification Value (CVV) verification.

Visa Chargeback

It is a dispute between a customer and a merchant regarding a purchase made with a Visa card. A chargeback occurs when a customer disputes a transaction and requests the funds be returned to their account. Visa acts as an intermediary between the cardholder's bank and the merchant's bank to resolve the dispute.

Visa Chargeback Monitoring Program

This is a program offered by Visa to help merchants manage their chargebacks more efficiently. It provides detailed reports, analysis, and notifications of chargeback activity and chargeback dispute deadlines.

Visa Chargeback Ratio

A Visa chargeback ratio is a metric used by Visa to measure a merchant's chargeback activity. A high chargeback ratio may affect a merchant's ability to conduct business and may result in fines or penalties.

Visa Chargeback Reason Codes

These are specific codes provided by Visa that describe the reason for a chargeback. They help merchants understand the underlying issue and take necessary corrective actions.

Visa Merchant Purchase Inquiry

Visa Merchant Purchase Inquiry (VMPI) is a program that allows merchants to proactively address customer complaints and prevent chargebacks. Merchants can respond to customer complaints using VMPI, reducing the likelihood of disputes and chargebacks.

Visa Resolve Online

It is a service provided by Visa used to resolve disputes between merchants and customers. Visa Resolve Online provides a platform for merchants to respond to chargeback requests made by cardholders. The service enables merchants to submit evidence and contest chargebacks.

Visa Secure

Visa Secure is a feature that adds an extra layer of security to online transactions. It requires cardholders to verify their identity before making a purchase, reducing the risk of fraud and chargebacks.

VisaNet

VisaNet is a global payment processing network used by Visa to handle credit and debit card transactions. It facilitates the exchange of information between merchants, cardholders, and financial institutions.

Vital

Vital is a payment processing company that provides payment solutions for businesses. It offers chargeback management tools that help merchants fight fraudulent chargebacks.

Voice Authorization

It is a manual process used by merchants to authorize credit card transactions by phone. Voice authorization is generally used when the credit card terminal is not working or if a card is not present. The merchant will need to provide the card information, the transaction amount, and relevant details to the voice authorization center to get approval

Void

A void transaction is one that is cancelled before its completion. In the context of credit card chargebacks, customers may initiate a chargeback for a void transaction if they were charged for it.

Void Transaction

It is a purchase or transaction that is cancelled, and no money is exchanged between the customer and the merchant. The funds are not debited from the customer's account nor credited to the merchant's account. The void can occur if the card is declined, if the purchase is no longer wanted, or if the transaction is processed incorrectly.

Voids and Refunds

A void is a cancelled transaction, while a refund is a reversal of a transaction that has already been completed. Customers may initiate chargebacks for voids and refunds if they are not properly processed by the merchant.

Warning Bulletin

A warning bulletin is a list of merchants who have had excessive chargebacks or fraudulent activity on their accounts. Merchants listed on a warning bulletin may have difficulty obtaining merchant services or may face higher fees and restrictions.

Warranties

Warranties are promises that a seller makes regarding the quality or condition of the product or service. In the case of chargebacks, if a customer files a chargeback claim due to a broken or defective product, having a warranty can help merchants dispute the claim and prove that they provided a functioning product.

Watch List

A watch list is a database of customers who have filed chargeback disputes in the past. Merchants can use watch lists to identify high-risk customers and potentially prevent future chargebacks by exercising extra caution when processing their orders.

Worldpay

Worldpay is a payment processing company that offers chargeback management services to merchants. Their services include dispute resolution, chargeback alerts, and chargeback tracking to help merchants minimize their chargeback risk.

Written Documentation

Written documentation, such as receipts or proof of delivery, can be crucial in a chargeback dispute. Merchants should keep detailed records of all transactions and communication with customers to provide evidence in their defense.

Wrongful Chargeback

A wrongful chargeback occurs when a customer disputes a legitimate transaction. Merchants can dispute these chargebacks with evidence of the transaction and attempt to recover their funds.

Y2K Chargeback

A Y2K Chargeback occurs when a customer disputes a credit card transaction made before the year 2000. This type of chargeback is rare, but they can still occur due to technical glitches or human error.

Y2K Compliance

Y2K Compliance refers to the readiness of a company's technology systems to handle the changeover from the year 1999 to 2000. Failure to ensure Y2K Compliance could result in operational and legal issues, including chargebacks.

Yadav Case

The Yadav Case was a landmark case in which an Indian merchant won against Chargeback fraud committed by dishonest customers. The case established a precedent that merchants can fight against fraudulent chargebacks by collecting evidence and disputing them.

Y-Chargeback

A Y-Chargeback happens when a customer files a chargeback with the credit card issuer instead of resolving the issue directly with the merchant. The letter "Y" indicates that the chargeback is caused by non-receipt of goods or services.

Y-Chargeback Reason Code

The Y-Chargeback Reason Code is used by credit card issuers to categorize the reason for a Y-Chargeback. The reason codes include non-receipt of goods or services, failure to cancel a recurring transaction, and duplicate processing.

Year-end Report

A Year-end Report is a summary of a merchant's business activity for the past year. The report includes information on sales, refunds, chargebacks, and other types of transactions that occurred during the year.

Year-to-Date Chargeback Ratio

The Year-to-Date Chargeback Ratio is a metric used by credit card issuers to evaluate merchant risk. It is calculated by dividing the total number of chargebacks in a year by the total number of transactions.

Yellow Alert

A Yellow Alert is a warning issued by a credit card issuer to a merchant when their chargeback ratio exceeds a certain threshold. This alert indicates that the merchant is at risk of being placed in the Chargeback Monitoring Program (CBMP).

Yellow Copy

The Yellow Copy is the copy of the sales invoice retained by the merchant when processing a credit card transaction. This copy is crucial in resolving disputes and chargebacks as it contains crucial information such as the cardholder signature and transaction date.

Yield Loss

Yield Loss refers to the amount of revenue that merchants lose as a result of chargebacks. It includes the cost of the goods, chargeback fees, and other expenses associated with managing chargebacks.